BIG
ANIMALS

ANNE PRIESTLEY

ILLUSTRATED BY IAN JACKSON

Kingfisher Books

Advisers: Mary Jane Drummond, Tutor in
Primary Education, Cambridge
Institute of Education, Cambridge
Iris Walkinshaw, Headteacher, Rushmore Infants
School, Hackney, London
Patricia Brown, Children's Librarian,
North Kensington Library, London

Technical adviser: Michael Chinery

The author and editor would also like to thank
Mark Priestley and Nora Clarke for their help in
the preparation of this book.

First published in 1987 by Kingfisher Books
Limited, Elsley Court, 20–22
Great Titchfield Street, London W1P 7AD
A Grisewood & Dempsey Company

BRITISH CATALOGUING IN PUBLICATION DATA
Priestley, Anne
Big animals.—(Stepping stones 4, 5, 6)
1. Animals—Juvenile literature
I. Title   II. Jackson, Ian *1960–*
III. Series
591   QL49
ISBN: 0 86272 249 7

Edited by Vanessa Clarke
Designed by Nicholas Cannan and David Nash
Cover designed by Pinpoint Design Company
Phototypeset by Southern Positives and Negatives
(SPAN), Lingfield, Surrey
Printed in Spain.

Contents

The animals in this book are all mammals. Mammals are a group of animals. All mammals drink milk when they are babies and have hair or fur on their bodies. Dogs and cats, hamsters and rabbits are mammals. Elephants and giraffes are mammals. So are people.

There are more than 800,000 kinds of insects in the world and more than 30,000 kinds of fishes. But there are only 5000 kinds of mammals.

BOXES
The boxes in this book give the weights and measurements of the biggest animals. These are the males.

4

Most mammals are smaller than people. Only a few kinds are really big. Big animals need so much food that they cannot live in fields or gardens. They can only find enough food to eat in much bigger places like grasslands and jungles.

This is a map of the world which shows where the animals in this book live. Most of them live in Africa where there is plenty of wild open space.

Other countries in the world do not have so many big animals because people have taken over the wild places. They have built houses and farms and cut down the trees.

In these countries big animals can live only in the places where people do not want to live. Tigers live in the jungles of India. Polar bears, moose and elephant seals live where it is very cold. Camels live in deserts where it is very dry. Bison live in huge parks which are kept wild just for them. And blue whales live in the oceans.

Moose

NORTH AMERICA

Bison

ATLANTIC OCEAN

SOUTH AMERICA

PACIFIC OCEAN

Elephant seal

ARCTIC

Polar bears also live in the north of North America.

Polar bear

EUROPE

ASIA

PACIFIC OCEAN

AFRICA

Camel

Tiger

ippo

Gorilla

Elephant

Giraffe

INDIAN OCEAN

AUSTRALIA

Rhino

Blue whale

ANTARCTICA

African elephants are the biggest animals on land. They have to spend 18 hours a day feeding because they are so big.

African elephants live in herds. There are female herds and male herds. The elephants bathing at this waterhole are females with their calves.

The leader of the herd has spotted danger. She spreads out her ears to make herself look bigger and more frightening. If a dangerous animal gets too close, she will charge with a great trumpeting roar.

AFRICAN ELEPHANT
Weighs up to 7000 kilogrammes.
About 3·5 metres tall.
About 6 metres long.
Lives up to 80 years.
Eats leaves, grass and bark.

Black rhinos are not really black. They are dark grey and usually covered in mud. They can hear and smell well but they cannot see very far.

This rhinoceros mother cannot see the lioness but she knows something is wrong because the tick birds are squawking and flapping around her head. The tick birds feed on the ticks and insects that burrow into the rhino's thick skin.

BLACK RHINOCEROS
Weighs about 4000 kilogrammes.
About 1·5 metres tall.
Eats leaves and roots.
Lives up to 50 years in zoos.

Hippos spend the daytime in rivers. It is often difficult to see them because they sink down under the water with just the tops of their heads showing. Sometimes they disappear altogether to move away along the river bottom. Hippos can stay under the water for nearly ten minutes.

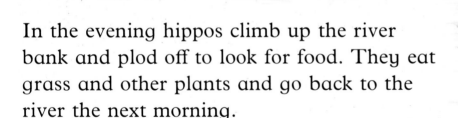

In the evening hippos climb up the river bank and plod off to look for food. They eat grass and other plants and go back to the river the next morning.

GIRAFFE
Tallest animal in the world; about 5·5 metres.
Babies are 1·5 metres tall at birth.
Weighs up to 1250 kilogrammes.
Lives up to 28 years in zoos.
Eats leaves and shoots.
Can gallop at about 45 kilometres an hour.

This giraffe is eating the leaves of an acacia tree. It avoids the sharp thorns by pulling down a twig with its long tongue. Then the giraffe picks off the leaves with its mouth.

Giraffes do not have to share their food with other animals because they are so tall. They can eat leaves and shoots that grow far above the heads of other animals.

Giraffes often feed and rest in clumps of acacia trees. It is difficult to see them among the trees because the squiggles and patches on their skin look like splashes of sunlight and shadow.

15

GORILLA
Weighs about 250
kilogrammes.
About 1·6 metres tall.
Eats leaves, shoots
and fruit.

This gorilla family has found a good place to camp for the night. But the biggest male does not sleep at night. He keeps watch.

If a leopard or other dangerous animal comes too close, he tries to frighten it away. He pulls up clumps of grass and throws them into the air. He hoots and beats his chest. He slaps the ground with his hands and jumps up and down. This is a terrifying sight but it is mostly pretence. Gorillas are very strong but they are also shy and gentle. They do not fight other animals if they can avoid it.

Many deserts are hot, dry, sandy places. There is little food or water. Most animals cannot live in deserts but camels can. They live in the deserts of northern Africa and the Middle East.

When a camel drinks, it can fill itself up with over 100 litres of water. When a camel eats, some of the food is turned into fat and stored in its hump. A camel can live for about 15 days without eating or drinking. It just uses up the store of fat in its hump and the water in its body.

ARABIAN CAMEL
Weighs up to 690 kilogrammes.
Up to 2 metres tall.
About 3 metres long.
Lives up to 50 years.
Eats grass and leaves.
Walks at 4 kilometres an hour.

18

People use camels to help them live in the desert. They use camels to carry things from one place to another. At the end of a long journey a camel is thin and its hump is small and floppy.

Camels do not sink into the sand because they have big padded feet. They have long eyelashes to protect their eyes and can close their nostrils to stop sand blowing in.

19

> **TIGER**
> Biggest cat.
> Weighs up to 225 kilogrammes.
> About 0·9 metres tall.
> About 3 metres long.
> Lives mostly in India.
> Eats the meat of deer and pigs; sometimes the meat of buffalo, frogs, rats and fish.

Tigers like to live and hunt on their own. They usually hunt at night because the pattern on their fur makes them difficult to see. In the moonlight the stripes look just like long grass and reeds.

This tiger is creeping up on a marsh deer. When it is close, it rushes forward. It knocks the deer to the ground with its huge front paws and kills it. The tiger eats as much meat as it can. Then it hides the rest to eat another day.

In this picture it is late summer. The female moose and her calves are eating water lilies at the side of a lake. The male moose has waded further in. He has huge antlers which he uses in autumn to fight other males. In spring the antlers fall off and he starts to grow another set. Only the males have antlers.

MOOSE
Biggest deer.
Weighs up to 700 kilogrammes.
About 2·3 metres tall.
Eats waterplants, grass, leaves, shoots and tree bark.
Moose live in North America; also in parts of Europe where they are called elk.

In summer, moose eat as much as they can and put on a thick layer of fat. They live off this fat through the winter when the ground is covered with snow and food is difficult to find.

The two male bison here are battling to find out which is the stronger. They charge each other, clash horns and push with their huge shoulders. The fight is over when one of them gives up and walks away.

Bison live in herds in North America. In the morning and evening they move slowly over the prairies eating grass. In the afternoon they lie down and rest. Bison also like dust baths. They roll and rub themselves in the dust and often make hollows in the ground.

This polar bear is hunting. It has seen a
seal sleeping on the ice and swims slowly
towards it. When it is close it leaps onto the
ice. Then it kills the seal with one blow from
its huge front paw.

Most polar bears spend all year hunting on
the ice. But at the beginning of winter
pregnant female bears dig dens deep into
the snow. They give birth to their cubs in
these dens and stay with them all winter. In
spring they come out to look for food.

POLAR BEAR
Weighs about 500 kilogrammes.
Babies weigh only 1 kilogramme at birth.
About 1·5 metres tall.
Lives up to 33 years in zoos.
Eats seals and birds.
Runs at up to 30 kilometres an hour.

27

ELEPHANT SEAL
Biggest seal.
Weighs up to 4000 kilogrammes.
About 6 metres long.
Females are only half as big as this.
Eats squid.
Also known as sea elephant.

These two male elephant seals are fighting. They bellow and roar through their trunk-like noses and hurl themselves at each other. When their bodies smack together they look like two giant quivering jellies.

The winner of this battle takes control of this part of the beach. He will fight other males who try to take it away from him.

The biggest animals in the world live in the sea. But they are not fishes. They are mammals like all the other animals in this book. They are called blue whales.

Blue whales live mostly in the colder parts of the world's oceans. They are very rare. There are probably only about 2000 of them left in the world.

You can see how huge blue whales are from this picture. They can weigh more than fifteen African elephants.

BLUE WHALE
Weighs up to 115,000 kilogrammes.
About 30 metres long.
Eats small shrimp-like animals called krill.
Can swim at 32 kilometres an hour in short bursts.

Index

Where to see big animals

You can see big animals in zoos and wildlife parks. To find out if there is one near you:

1 Look up **ZOO** in the telephone directory.
2 Ask at your library.
3 Look through the advertisements in a local newspaper.